Self Discipline
The Ultimate Guide to Achieve Success in Business, Relationships, and Life with Unbreakable Habits, Navy Seal Mental Toughness, and a Monk Mindset for Increased Productivity
Eric Holt

Copyright © 2023 by Eric Holt

All rights reserved.

It is not legal to reproduce, duplicate, or transmit any part of this document in either electronic means or in printed format. Recording of this publication is strictly prohibited and any storage of this document is not allowed unless with written permission from the publisher except for the use of brief quotations in a book review.

ISBN: 9781835123294

Contents

Introduction   V

1. Understanding Self-Discipline   1
   What Is Self-Discipline, And Why Is It Important?
   Overcoming Common Misconceptions About Self-Discipline

2. Building Unbreakable Habits   9
   The Science Behind Habits
   How Habits Influence Our Daily Lives
   What Are Bad Habits?
   A Comparison Of Good And Bad Habits
   Examples Of Bad Habits
   How To Break Bad Habits
   Strategies To Develop Positive Habits

3. Navy SEAL Mental Toughness   19
   Exploring The Mindset Of Navy SEALs
   How Are Navy SEALs So Mentally Tough?
   Why Are Navy SEALs So Unique?
   What Is The Most Important Trait Navy SEAL?
   How Do I Get The Mental Strength Of A Navy SEAL?
   Techniques To Overcome Obstacles And Stay Focused

Free Goodwill   32

4. Cultivating A Monk Mindset   34

Understanding The Principles Of A Monk's Mindset
Practices To Achieve Mental Clarity And Reduce Stress
Balancing Productivity With Mindfulness And Presence

5. Strengthening Self-Discipline In Business   46
Building The Necessary Discipline To Become An Entrepreneur
Strategies For Effective Time Management And Goal Setting

6. Mastering Self-Discipline In Relationships   53
The Importance Of Self-Discipline In Relationships
Communication Skills To Build Strong Connections

7. Sustaining Self-Discipline For Life - Embracing   61
The Journey
Maintaining Discipline In The Face Of Distractions
Strategies For Self-Reflection And Continuous Improvement
Career Milestones To Celebrate

Conclusion   71

Introduction

For many, self-discipline is a bright target on the horizon, a time when we ultimately master our chaotic, flawed selves. With the help of self-discipline, I will finally be able to maintain my goals (stop eating sugar, get out every morning, learn a new language) and realize my dreams.

It serves as a yardstick by which we assess our character, activities, and ourselves in the eyes of others. We often mistake it for willpower. (Typically, we fall short).

Discipline-building is a practice, not a goal or a benchmark. Although practice never ends, we do improve our skills.

Many people try to be disciplined, yet it's more difficult than we think to become disciplined. Our mental health, upbringing, personal habits, and current situations influence our ability to handle ourselves.

Like self-love or addressing our anxieties requires careful effort, learning to be disciplined does too. Even though it can appear to be an impossible dragon, improvement is always attainable. You can acquire the self-discipline that matters for you and your goals through practice by learning to work within the constraints of who you are and what you have.

The key to good leadership for yourself and others is discipline. Focus and self-discipline lead to contentment, happiness, and success. When faced with an all-you-can-eat buffet, the chance to make quick cash, or the sleepy allure of staying in rather than joining the Peloton, it may not be easy to believe, but studies show that those with self-discipline are happier. Why? Because when we exercise self-control and discipline, we achieve more of the goals that are most important to us. The link between set goals and goals achieved is self-discipline.

Self-discipline experts spend less time pondering whether to engage in actions and behaviors inconsistent with their values or goals. They make better decisions. They resist letting emotions or impulses guide their decisions. They are the designers of their thoughts and the steps they take to achieve a desired result. As a result, they are less susceptible to being sidetracked by temptation and exhibit higher levels of life satisfaction.

You can follow certain steps to develop self-discipline and the willpower necessary to lead a happier, more fulfilled life. Here are the most effective things you can do to acquire self-discipline, which is essential for living outside your comfort zone, and perhaps even redefining "extraordinary."

1
Understanding Self-Discipline

Be honest for a moment. For the majority of us, developing self-discipline is a process that is hampered by good intentions, procrastination, and failure-related emotions. But it shouldn't have to be.

Instead of putting your phone down and going to bed, you continue to play Candy Crush. Fortunately, you can retrain your brain to follow your commands by employing specific psychological strategies.

Self-discipline is a skill that must be developed. Even while you won't have a perfect practice day every day, you will still get closer to your objective with each day's failures and little accomplishments. This chapter provides tips on how to use self-discipline in everyday life.

What Is Self-Discipline, And Why Is It Important?

Self-discipline is the capacity to carry out what your brain says is the proper course of action in spite of bodily resistance.

Self-discipline often entails deferring your comfort or urges in favor of long-term achievement. For instance, you might need to consciously eliminate distractions like canceling your Netflix subscription to read more.

A great strategy to manage stress and anxiety is to play a self-disciplined role. Self-discipline can offer a variety of advantages.

Ten benefits of self-discipline are listed below.

1. More Effective Time Management

The ability to better manage your time is one of the biggest advantages of self-discipline. Everybody has a never-ending list of things to do, which makes us feel anxious, irritable, and emotionally spent. However, you'll find that you have more free time and feel less stressed if you can manage your task well and concentrate on one thing at a time.

When you have self-discipline, you become more organized and can easily prioritize your daily tasks. Making time management a habit over time will prevent you from rushing through tasks, which will relieve some of your stress and worry. Being disciplined makes it easier to manage your time.

2. More Efficiency

Being more productive is another advantage of exercising self-discipline. Every day, you feel more successful and content with your life as you can accomplish more. Additionally, productivity helps you feel peaceful after completing your responsibilities, preventing stress or anxiety when things aren't accomplished.

Perhaps you want to advance professionally. By completely focusing on your task, self-discipline can help you swiftly accomplish more with less, preventing procrastination and frustration. Additionally, your supervisors will probably notice your productivity, success at work, and happiness.

3. Enhanced Interactions

You can concentrate on your relationships when completing tasks, working efficiently, and having more free time. You won't have to postpone or cancel plans you make with family and friends, and you'll be able to spend time with them without feeling obligated to do something else.

When you are dissatisfied, stressed out, or believe you don't have enough time, your relationships may become strained. By practicing self-discipline, you can exert more control over your tasks and ensure you have time for important people. Spending time with people is important for socialization, so do it.

4. Put Your Mind At Ease

The ability to regulate your thoughts is the main advantage of self-discipline. By setting a vision for yourself and taking deliberate actions to get there, you give yourself more clarity to set out and accomplish your goals. You can free yourself of distractions and change your perspective to give yourself the credit you deserve. There is no need to serve anyone else.

Use optimistic language when you speak and try to push away any doubt or negativity as much as possible as realistic and easy steps to enhance your thinking. With the boosts of positivity, you can concentrate on efficiently guiding your thoughts to be more optimistic and believe more in yourself and your potential.

5. Providing Self-Care For Yourself

Making time for oneself might be difficult, but self-care is crucial to our wellbeing. With self-discipline, you can emphasize scheduling "me time" and learning to say "no" when something interferes. You take charge of how your time is used to guarantee that you give yourself the attention you need.

For instance, schedule some downtime if your schedule is getting busier. Perhaps you might spend a few minutes each morning in appreciation and meditation. You might also consider setting aside a few days each week to take a bubble bath or relax with a good book.

To ensure you are routinely practicing more self-care, consider what makes you happy and peaceful and try to incorporate them into your week. As a result, you'll feel more at ease, refreshed, and prepared to take on your next task.

6. Inspire Confidence

"How can I be more confident" is a frequent question on Google about self-discipline. When you practice self-discipline, you give yourself the ability to carry out your goals, and when you succeed, your confidence is boosted. You start to believe that you can do more and do more while experiencing less stress and anxiety.

7. You Improve Your Physical And Mental Health

Your emotional and physical health will benefit from incremental progress toward your health goals. For instance, if you begin each day with meditation and exercise and gradually increase the frequency from a few days a week to five or more, you will discover that you have empowered yourself to lead a healthy life.

8. You Develop Resistance

You might believe that starting something doesn't need much work. Self-discipline, conversely, carries out the commitment and effort to continue the task over time. The secret is persistence, which you develop through self-discipline practice and allows you the resilience to maintain despite setbacks or difficulties.

9. Making Improved Decisions

Sometimes you make snap judgments you regret because they weren't well thought through. The ability to manage your behavior comes from self-discipline, and developing good habits can help you make better-informed decisions by allowing you more time to think over your options.

Imagine, for example, that you are exercising more restraint when it comes to your eating habits. Making time to meal prep to provide healthy options and prepare nourishing meals is a small step to assist yourself in achieving that goal.

All too often, it is easy to get caught up in your hectic schedule and grab takeout or fast food because you are pressed for time and forget to make your meals. Instead, start by preparing food for a few breakfasts or lunches and then progress to preparing nutritious dinners. Your goals will become more realistic by taking smaller measures.

10. Increased Standards

The realization that you deserve wonderful things is one of the last advantages of self-discipline to mention. You can uphold your principles, provide long-term benefits, and refuse to accept anything less. Rising standards enable you to succeed by overcoming hurdles and paving the path for a better, brighter future.

Overcoming Common Misconceptions About Self-Discipline

One of those topics that no one loves to discuss or learn about is self-discipline, even though we all know we need it. Sometimes the term itself causes us to shudder. Maybe this is because most people falsely understand what self-discipline is and isn't.

Self-discipline is typically viewed as a type of punishment since, in our minds, it involves doing what you don't want to do when you don't want to. Yet it isn't.

People's perceptions of self-discipline have a negative connotation because of four common misconceptions.

Self-Discipline Is Selective

We usually view it as a noun, which denotes that some people have it while others do not. Because it makes individuals think that they are out of luck if they have trouble making moral decisions because the fairy of self-discipline has passed them by, this notion is self-defeating.

In spite of the fact that the term is listed as a noun in every important dictionary, my expertise leads me to believe that it is actually more closely related to a verb. Self-discipline is more of a tool than a goal in and of itself. Many of the 2,700 clients we've counseled acknowledge having issues with self-discipline. But as we engage with them, we see that their issue is less about self-discipline and more about a lack of vision. No matter who you are, if you can improve someone's self-discipline (v.), you will instantly observe a boost in their eyesight (n.).

Self-Discipline Is Difficult

Those who don't understand self-discipline are the only ones with this mentality. A hard life is not the result of self-discipline. Being devoid of it is. While challenging short-term decisions have direct long-term effects. What appears to be the simple solution—eating whatever we want, speaking whatever we feel like, and purchasing anything we want on credit—makes life more challenging.

Exercising self-discipline isn't as difficult as we might believe when we know how to think about it appropriately. Like everything new, self-discipline is initially unfamiliar and takes some getting used to. But once your brain forms the neural pathways for particular decisions, self-control comes naturally and without thought. You cease seeing indulgences as alternatives because you understand that they are nothing more than debtors who charge you interest, and as a result, their influence over you starts to wane. It gets easier to resist temptation the longer you resist it.

Self-Discipline Lacks Emotions

People who believe self-discipline requires an iron will and muscular power are completely mistaken. Understanding, analyzing, and managing your emotions is the lovely art of self-discipline. Self-discipline is not about brute force but grace, understanding, subtlety, and strength.

Additionally, exercising self-discipline does not entail denying oneself anything positive. It just entails intentionally using your heart and mind to direct how you live. Remember that having self- discipline doesn't just mean being able to stick to a strict diet or work out like a beast. It has to do with how intuitively you comprehend how your own heart and intellect interact. Your capacity to persuade others will grow tremendously as you better understand and control your emotions. Perhaps where self-discipline has the biggest impact is in our ability to communicate with others.

Self-Control Is Boring

Most of the time, when we hear the word "self-discipline," we think of salads, weightlifting, getting into trouble, and self-discipline. But I can guarantee you that self-discipline is much more frequently linked with things like riches, sex, hotness, influence, peace, joy, and spirit than it is with anything else after spending almost ten years studying the most successful and disciplined people on the planet.

What is self-discipline then? The ability to read and control one's emotions so as to further one's goals in life is the art, science, and skill of self-discipline. Discipline is not "doing what you don't want to do when you don't want to do it."

2
Building Unbreakable Habits

Habits are habitual, routine behaviors or acts we carry out without realizing them. They develop over time as our brains forge stronger neural connections each time we behave. This chapter will look at habits and how they impact our daily lives and give instances of good and bad habits.

The Science Behind Habits

The habit loop, a three-stage method for forming habits, includes the following steps:

- **Cue** - This is the habit's triggering event. It might be a particular moment in time, a place, a feeling, or other people.

- **Routine** - The actual behavior or action you take in response to the cue is your routine.

- **Reward** - This is the favorable result or advantage

that strengthens the habit and increases the likelihood that it will be repeated.

The neural circuits connected to the habit strengthen over time when the habit loop is repeated, making the practice more automatic and challenging to break.

How Habits Influence Our Daily Lives

Our habits significantly shape our daily lives. They can affect our relationships, productivity, and health, among other areas.

Health

Our habits can greatly impact our mental and physical state. For instance, healthy behaviors like regular exercise and a balanced diet can improve general health and lower the risk of developing chronic diseases. On the other hand, bad habits like smoking, drinking too much alcohol, and getting little sleep can harm our health and wellbeing.

For instance, running

Jane has developed the practice of running every morning before work. She now has better cardiovascular health, better control over her weight, and more energy throughout the day.

Productivity

In both our personal and professional life, our habits directly impact how productive and effective we are. For instance, developing good time management practices like prioritizing work and blocking off specific periods for concentrated work can greatly increase productivity.

For instance, The Pomodoro Technique.

The Pomodoro Technique, a time-management strategy that divides work into intervals of typically 25 minutes, followed by a brief break, has been used by many. This increases productivity and the capacity to concentrate without being overburdened.

Relationships

Additionally, our interpersonal connections are significantly shaped by our habits. Effective communication techniques can promote deeper relationships and assist in dispute resolution, such as active listening and expressing gratitude. Negative behaviors, such as excessive screen time or a lack of empathy, can strain relationships.

For instance, weekly date night

Every week, Susan and John have a date night where they intentionally connect and communicate. Due to this behavior, they have a stronger link and are more aware of one another's wants and needs.

What Are Bad Habits?

Any behavior that we engage in frequently enough to feel almost automatic is referred to as a habit. We might classify this tendency as a "bad habit" if it becomes unwanted.

According to the dictionary, a bad habit is "a patterned behavior thought to be harmful to one's mental or physical health, often linked to a lack of self-discipline." A poor habit is a repetitive behavior that usually gives you short-term satisfaction but often causes long-term issues.

For instance, one of the ways I used to manage my stress while in graduate school was to indulge in internet shopping occasionally. It wasn't a huge issue initially, but it became a habit after some time, and I had difficulty making my credit card payments. Fortunately, I caught it before I racked up too much debt, but I can state with certainty that retail therapy is one of my bad habits.

A Comparison Of Good And Bad Habits

Our brain doesn't have to work as hard when we develop habits. We link the trigger, the action, and the reward, but we may not always link the long-term effects. For instance, if you know that smoking a cigarette will help you relax, you'll keep doing it until it becomes second nature (or a habit). Although bad habits like this may feel enjoyable in the short term, they have detrimental long-term physical, emotional, and psychological effects.

Bad habits have the following traits: they can make you feel guilty or unhappy, keep you up at night, or negatively impact your health. Good habits, on the other hand, have beneficial long-term impacts. We know, for instance, that going for a morning walk can improve your cardiovascular health, mood, and mental well-being. Examples of healthy habit traits are building a routine that supports excellent health, including self-care, and elevating self-esteem.

Examples Of Bad Habits

Here are a few of the undesirable behaviors that humans most often exhibit.

- **Smoking-** Research has shown that smoking is unhealthy, even in small amounts. The advantages of quitting, however, start happening just 20 minutes after your last smoke.

- **Not Working Out** - This bad habit is less visible than smoking, which is blatantly unhealthy for you. However, bad habits can occasionally be inaction. You should exercise for both your physical and emotional wellness. To get a healthy half hour of exercise each day, it could be best to start by exercising for short periods, such as 15 minutes in the morning and 15 minutes after work.

- **Lacking Sufficient Sleep** - Life is impossible without sleep. According to research, sleep deprivation has been connected to an increased risk of heart attack, diabetes, stroke, obesity, depression, and high blood pressure. You might want to remember that the average grown-up needs more than 7 hours of sleep every night while creating your timetable. If you have trouble falling asleep, you might want to talk to your doctor about it.

- **Using Screens For Too Long Before Night** - Breaking the habit of gazing at a screen immediately before bed is one approach to getting better sleep. According to several studies, the light emitted by electronics like TVs, tablets, and smartphones can interfere with the hormones that make us fall asleep. Instead, practicing mindfulness meditation or reading before bed may be beneficial.

- **Slouching** - Many of us today have jobs requiring us to sit in front of a computer screen or at a desk for one reason or another. Lower back pain might result from slouching or hunching too regularly. Correcting your posture or occasionally getting up and strolling about your workspace could be beneficial.

- **Overspending** - Buying items we don't necessarily need is one of the common ways we deal with stress. If left unchecked, it can easily result in people going into debt; thus, it may be helpful to create a budget or establish a strategy to check your accounts frequently to prevent this.

- **Procrastination** - We often don't give ourselves enough time to complete our plans, and I know I'm guilty of it. People tend to put things off because they are either perfectionists or lazy. Creating (and adhering to) a schedule to get things done on time may be helpful.

- **Negative Inner Dialogue** - Too many people cannot compliment themselves. We as a people are often encouraged to be our own worst critics, which may occasionally become debilitating and result in low self-esteem. Since encouraging yourself can help you see the positive side of things and eventually make you feel better, using positive self-talk is a good idea.

How To Break Bad Habits

How do we break bad habits now that we know what they are and what causes them? Certain people may advise you to stop simply, but that is easier said than done.

The following actions could help you in kicking bad habits:

- **Find The Bad Habit -** You might wish to identify the specific habit that you want to change. You may know smoking is unhealthy, but what are some workable alternatives? You might wish to cease taking as many smoke breaks at work, switch to nicotine patches or other alternatives, or both.

- **Find Out What Triggers You -** You might want to consider why your bad habit is so compelling. What led you to form the habit, and what keeps you returning? Simple things like seeing snacks on the kitchen counter may encourage you to eat when you're bored; putting them in the cabinets may help you avoid overindulging. Emotional triggers might occasionally start our bad habits. Is it stress, fatigue, or boredom? When determining what triggers your bad habit, take these factors into account.

- **Eliminate As Many Triggers As Possible -** Focusing on the triggers themselves might help you change your behavioral habit. Triggers are the occasions that set off your brain's automatic drive to carry out the habit. This might be anything in our environment that our brain has connected to a certain habit. These triggers, such as the people you were with and the environment, might have a subtle but significant impact on your habit. Put those goodies away in advance, or if your poor habit is emotional, look for strategies to enhance your mental well-being. To relax more, you can practice deep breathing and meditation, or you might seek professional assistance.

- **Replace The Bad Habit** - Research now demonstrates that just quitting or discontinuing a bad habit is ineffective. You formed the habit for a cause, and it gave relief or satiated a need. Instead, replacing your bad habit with a good, or at least a better one, might be more fruitful. However, how the new habit makes you feel is more important than its specifics. Feeling good about your decisions and your new habit would be the aim. You want to be certain that the new habit won't make you feel poorly about yourself.

- **Get Help** - Finding others trying to kick the same bad habit may be helpful. Groups that get together to stop drinking, smoking, or engaging in other vices could offer moral and emotional support. This might make it easier for you to keep your word and provide someone to share your successes with. Another powerful motivator is realizing someone is counting on you to improve.

- **Visualize Success** - Close your eyes and visualize yourself removing junk food and cigarettes from the house. Imagine getting up early or going for a run after work. Whatever your bad habit is, seeing yourself conquering it and reveling in your accomplishment can be inspiring.

- **Keep Trying, But Be Patient** - You might make mistakes occasionally, and change takes time. Although nobody is perfect, success depends on being consistent. New brain connections and habits can emerge over time. Don't be too hard on yourself when you make mistakes; simply focus on each day.

Strategies To Develop Positive Habits

You can start creating a healthier lifestyle and learn to regulate your desires by learning how to create new habits and eliminate negative ones. Consider the following advice for creating positive habits:

- **Goals Should Be Written Down** - Write down the bad habits you wish to stop and the good ones you want to develop. Use post-it notes to attach reminders of your goals to surfaces where you aim to create new habits, such as your office desk, refrigerator, or bathroom mirror.

- **Prevent Triggers** - Eliminating the habits, people, and environments that initially set off the harmful habit is the key to breaking it. Consider going to a less tempting store if, for instance, you often overspend at a certain supermarket store.

- **Determine The Underlying Reason For Your Habits** - Your response to desires determines how habits are formed. Cravings are often triggered. Your brain uses triggers as a means of attracting rewards. Making better judgments and breaking poor habits might be easier by knowing the reward you seek. For instance, even though a healthier choice might help you feel better, you might reach for fried foods to deal with a stressful day. Knowing what your body or mind is craving might help you exercise greater restraint and make choices that will help you form healthy habits.

- **Be Sure To Make Just Small Changes** - Building a new habit or changing an established one can be difficult. By beginning with small modifications, you can modify your daily routine in a significant way. Concentrate on developing small, consistent routines. For instance, take five daily walks if you want to start working out more.

- **Create A Daily Schedule** - One of the most effective strategies for changing your habit is consistency. Choose a time of day to practice them and stick to it once you've decided on whatever healthy habits you want to adopt.

- **Track Your Development** - It's crucial to monitor your development when trying to acquire new habits. You can accomplish this by utilizing habit-tracking software or a journal. Measuring your development enables you to appreciate little victories and maintains your motivation.

- **Identify A Partner For Accountability** - A support system can improve your chances of creating long-lasting habit modification. Ask a close friend, family member, coach, or mentor to keep you accountable for the behavior change you want.

3
Navy SEAL Mental Toughness

Navy SEALs are some of the world's toughest people. Additionally, they can teach us something.

One of the world's most mentally strong people, the US Navy SEALs are known for their resilience. The Navy SEALs always work in situations where regular combat groups are often unable to succeed. In these situations, the Navy SEALs must exercise the highest mental toughness and teamwork while working in environments ordinary people cannot fathom. This distinguishes the resilience of the Navy SEALs.

Do you know what's truly fascinating? Finding out how Navy SEALs develop their mental toughness to deal with dangerous situations.

The best part is that we can apply these techniques to improve our work and personal performance. Let's see how.

Exploring The Mindset Of Navy SEALs

The crucial qualities, abilities, and attitudes that make up "The Navy Seal Mindset" make them successful. People can achieve their goals and overcome challenges in many areas of life by adopting and applying this mindset. People can attain their goals and overcome challenges in all facets of life by properly putting these skills to use.

We'll discuss the Navy Seal Mindset's strength and how you may use it to achieve your goals.

<u>Mental Resilient</u>

Mental resilience is one of the defining characteristics of the Navy Seal Mindset. This is the capacity to rise beyond obstacles, failures, and hardship. Never giving up, Navy Seals push themselves to their absolute physical and mental boundaries. To fully utilize the power of the Navy Seal Mindset, you must cultivate mental toughness by viewing obstacles and failures as chances to improve.

<u>Focus</u>

Navy Seals must keep their focus in high-pressure situations where even the smallest mistake could mean the difference between life and death. To fully utilize the Navy Seal Mindset, you must learn to concentrate on your goals and avoid distractions. This entails selecting priorities for your time and effort, establishing specific goals, and pursuing them tenaciously.

<u>Perseverance</u>

A key component of the Navy Seal Mindset is perseverance. The Navy Seals continue to work despite their discomfort, tiredness, and pain. You must cultivate perseverance by establishing difficult goals, pushing yourself outside your comfort zone, and never giving up if you want to use the power of the Navy Seal Mindset.

Adaptability

The ability to adapt and make quick decisions under pressure is a need for Navy Seals. They are taught to anticipate and react to changes in their surroundings and swiftly change their plans. You must cultivate adaptability by being open to change, remaining flexible, and learning to improvise when necessary to utilize the Navy Seal Mindset's potential fully.

Discipline

The Navy Seal Mindset is dependent on discipline. The rigorous regulations and procedures that Navy Seals must always adhere to are taught to them. Create a plan, make clear goals, and adhere to it with consistency and attention to detail to develop discipline.

Teamwork

Finally, the Navy Seal Mindset places a strong emphasis on teamwork. Each member of the closely coordinated teams that the Navy Seals work in is essential to the mission's success. Work well in teams using your communication, support, and contributing skills to adopt the Navy Seal Mindset.

Navy Seal Mindset: strong characteristics, abilities, and attitudes to accomplish goals and overcome challenges. To fully utilize the potential of the Navy Seal Mindset, develop resilience, focus, perseverance, adaptability, discipline, and teamwork. Determine your areas of weakness, and then consciously cultivate your strengths. You, too, can achieve your goals by using the Navy Seal Mindset with patience and practice.

How Are Navy SEALs So Mentally Tough?

The mental toughness of Navy SEALs helps them in overcoming difficult and hazardous circumstances. What, though, gives Navy SEALs their exceptional mental toughness? This section examines some major elements that influence Navy SEALs' mental toughness.

Rigorous Training

The most rigorous training available to any military organization is given to the Navy SEALs. Their training pushes them to their physical and mental limitations to prepare them for tough situations. Exercises like running, swimming, and calisthenics are a part of SEAL training, along with more complicated techniques like underwater demolition and specific weapons training. By educating SEALs to persevere through pain and weariness and never to give up, this demanding training helps to develop mental toughness.

High-Stress Situations

The stakes are often life or death when Navy SEALs operate in high-stress situations. The frequent stress that SEALs experience teaches them how to control their emotions and remain composed under pressure, which helps to develop mental toughness. SEALs receive training to retain mental clarity and concentration even in the most trying circumstances.

Setting Goals

Clear goals and a strategy for achieving them are skills that Navy SEALs learn. This gives SEALs a sense of purpose and direction, which aids in developing mental toughness. SEALs learn to overcome barriers and accomplish their goals by setting difficult goals and pursuing them with tenacity and focus.

In conclusion, hard training, mental toughness, stressful environments, goal-setting, and teamwork all contribute to the Navy SEALs' exceptional mental toughness. These elements combine to produce a mindset emphasizing perseverance and the capacity to overcome even the most difficult difficulties. While not everyone has the potential to become a Navy SEAL, everyone can work to improve their mental toughness by accepting challenges, creating specific goals, and discovering effective stress and adversity management techniques. You can increase your mental toughness and accomplish your goals by emulating some Navy SEALs' methods and attitudes.

Why Are Navy SEALs So Unique?

The Navy SEALs are the most disciplined fighting forces in the world. They are an invincible force due to their strength on the battlefield, mental toughness, and steadfast dedication to their goal. This section examines what makes Navy SEALs unique and how they differ from other military branches.

Specialization

The skills and abilities used by Navy SEALs are extremely specialized. They receive training to function in various settings, such as land, sea, and air. SEALs are additionally skilled with firearms, hand-to-hand fighting, and explosives.

SEALs can thrive in various tasks, from hostage rescue to surveillance, because of their specialization.

<u>Commitment</u>

Last but not least, Navy SEALs exhibit an unshakeable dedication to their objective. They are prepared to risk their lives to serve their country and fulfill their obligations. The dedication of SEALs to their teams and missions is seen in everything they do, including their rigorous training.

Navy SEALs are unique due to their in-depth training, specialization, ability to function in high-stress situations, teamwork, and steadfast dedication to their goal. Due to these characteristics, SEALs are among the most efficient and well-respected military groups in the entire world. While not everyone has what it takes to become a Navy SEAL, we can all benefit from their commitment, collaboration, and determination to become better versions of ourselves. We can accomplish our goals and change the world if we acquire some of the same traits and mindsets as Navy SEALs.

What Is The Most Important Trait Navy SEAL?

What distinguishing quality helps Navy SEALs succeed in their missions? Here, we'll look at the answer to this question and delve further into the characteristics that define a Navy SEAL.

Many current and former Navy SEALs see resilience as the most important quality, according to interviews with numerous of them. Already using the active voice in this statement. No adjustments are required. Navy SEALs must possess this ability because they often work in risky, high-stress conditions.

Navy SEALs who possess resilience can persevere when times are bad. It enables people to continue concentrating on their goal in the face of discomfort, tiredness, and anxiety. This trait enables SEALs to adjust to shifting circumstances and creatively respond to unforeseen difficulties.

Resilience, though, is more than just mental tenacity. It also encompasses the capacity for good teamwork, communication, and adaptability. Because Navy SEALs are highly specialized and work in small teams, getting along with others and being flexible when circumstances change is essential.

In addition to resilience, the following qualities are crucial for being a great Navy SEAL:

- **Leadership** - Navy SEALs are taught to take command of situations when necessary and to be leaders. This necessitates the capacity for swift decision-making, good communication, and confidence-building in others.

- **Discipline** - Navy SEALs are disciplined in everyday routines and physical training. Thanks to this discipline, they can keep their mental and physical toughness, which also helps them stay focused on their objectives.

- **Humility** - Despite being among the best, Navy SEALs are humble and aware of their limitations. They can take criticism well, learn from their mistakes, and continually strive for improvement because of their humility.

- **Perseverance** - The Navy SEALs are renowned for their never-quit mentality. They are prepared to exert themselves to the absolute limit and to persevere in the face of adversity.

In conclusion, even though Navy SEALs have a variety of vital qualities that contribute to their success, resilience is probably the most crucial. Thanks to resilience, they can continue moving forward and remaining focused on their goals. However, Navy SEALs exhibit other vital qualities, including tenacity, leadership, discipline, and humility. We can improve and accomplish our goals by learning and incorporating these traits into our daily lives.

How Do I Get The Mental Strength Of A Navy SEAL?

Navy SEALs have shown incredible resiliency and mental toughness. These elite warriors go through some of the world's hardest and most demanding training regimens, which aids in developing an unmatched capacity to remain focused, retain composure, and persevere even under the most trying conditions.

But how can we achieve the same resiliency and mental toughness as a Navy SEAL? Here, we'll look at some of the most effective tactics and methods employed by Navy SEALs to maintain their mental toughness and provide tips on how you may implement these ideas in your own life.

Develop A Positive Mindset

A positive mindset is one of the most crucial elements to being mentally strong, like a Navy SEAL. Instead of focusing on the negative, Navy SEALs are taught to concentrate on the positive parts of a scenario. Even in the face of difficulty, they are taught to reframe negative beliefs and maintain optimism.

Concentrate on your accomplishments and strengths rather than your flaws to cultivate a positive mindset. You can cultivate gratitude by setting aside time each day to think of your blessings. Additionally, avoid becoming bogged down by circumstances you cannot control and concentrate on what you can control.

Set Clear Goals

Setting definite goals is a crucial component of mental toughness. The Navy SEALs are extremely focused and clearly understand their goals. They divide their goals into manageable, smaller tasks and concentrate on achieving each one successfully.

Start by establishing specific, attainable goals to acquire this skill. Make a plan to accomplish them after you have written them down. Make sure your goals are demanding yet attainable, and never forget to recognize and appreciate your accomplishments as you go.

Develop Your Resiliency

One of the basic traits of Navy SEALs is resilience, a quality you can acquire with practice. Start by accepting challenges head-on and not running from challenging circumstances. Accept failure as a chance to develop and learn rather than something to be feared.

Try to embrace discomfort and regularly push yourself if you want to develop resilience. Don't be scared to push yourself beyond your comfort zone, both physically and emotionally, and don't give up when things become tough. Keep in mind that failures and setbacks are a normal part of learning.

Concentrate On The Present Moment

The capacity to be present and concentrate on the work at hand is one of the most crucial components of mental toughness. Navy SEALs are taught to focus on the now rather than the past or future.

Try practicing mindfulness meditation to hone this skill. This entails concentrating on your breath and returning your attention to the here and now anytime your mind wanders. This can assist you in becoming more conscious of your thoughts and feelings and maintain your present-moment focus.

Develop A Network Of Allies

Finally, having a solid support system is among the most crucial elements in achieving mental toughness. The sense of togetherness that results from functioning as a tight-knit unit is something that Navy SEALs primarily rely on.

Try to surround yourself with supportive, upbeat individuals who will inspire you and keep you motivated as you develop your support network. Don't hesitate to ask for assistance; contact friends and family for support.

In conclusion, even if Navy SEAL training and experiences are unique, we can still use the same principles and strategies they employ to build mental toughness and resilience in our own lives. We can become psychologically stronger and more resilient like a Navy SEAL by cultivating a good mentality, establishing specific goals, practicing resilience, staying present, and creating a support system.

Techniques To Overcome Obstacles And Stay Focused

Even the best of us encounters obstacles to accomplishing our educational goals, and we are left wondering how to get beyond them. However, whether it's a challenging course, family issues, illness, or a lack of study time, it's possible to overcome them and come out on the other side stronger than before and even closer to accomplishing your goals.

The best techniques to stay focused on your goals even when challenges make them seem unattainable are listed below:

Prepare For Potential Problems By Anticipating Them

Set both long-term and short-term goals that are attainable and realistic. Next, list any potential roadblocks (such as problems with your family, finances, health, or other factors) and consider how they would affect your development if they materialized. Third, list the resources you could use to overcome each probable difficulty. Fourth, realize that everyone requires support occasionally, so speak with your advisers and teachers to explain the situation and ask for help. Make use of the resources you've located and seek assistance! Don't let pride get in the way of your accomplishment.

Establish Specific Goals And Update Them As Necessary

Make a goal or to-do list, and make sure your goals are reasonable. I use this both personally and professionally. Decide what you want to achieve in the end. Make a list of tasks you need to complete to reach that goal. Set deadlines for when you want to complete the goal and timeframes for each task. Put it up where it will be seen every day. Recognize that you will experience setbacks. Don't let them depress you too much. When they do, go back to your goals and make any necessary revisions to any task or goals. Finally, don't be averse to seeking assistance. Any obstacles you encounter will be easier to overcome with a solid support system.

Look For An Accountability Partner

The path to achieving your goals is never simple, and difficulties will inevitably arise! It's critical to have a strategy to help overcome these obstacles. I prefer to create small goals to ensure I'm completing what I need along the route. Additionally, I advise having a strong supporter nearby who can help you overcome any obstacles and hold you accountable while keeping you on track. You don't have to handle this by yourself! Having strong support and minor targets will keep your goals in mind.

Keep A Journal As You Work Through The Issue

What lesser goals must you complete to accomplish your main goal? You can gain more understanding of what might need to change in your path by journaling your progress toward those minor milestones and then reflecting on them (weekly, monthly, etc.). For example, weight loss: If you want to lose weight (say, 10 pounds), one of your minor goals might be to reduce your daily calorie intake from x to y. Maintaining a daily food journal can help you stay on track for accomplishing and sustaining that smaller milestone, which will ultimately help you reach your final goal.

Reframe Challenges As Chances For Learning

Recognize that someone will always stand in the way of your achievement and try to thwart it. Make sure that person is not you! On the way to success, we should all be prepared for obstacles. They might make you go more slowly but do not alter your course. The inverse of the adage, "What would you try if you believed you couldn't fail? " is to use every challenge as a teaching opportunity."

Free Goodwill

Dear seeker of self-discipline,

Before we start a chapter about how to cultivate a monk mindset, I want to recognize your dedication to personal development and your strong desire to succeed in everything you do—business, relationships, and every other aspect of your life. You have already made a significant stride by accepting self-discipline as the cornerstone of your ascent to greatness.

I now invite you to share your inspiring journey and wisdom with those who desire to discipline themselves and undergo profound life changes. Your life experiences and sage advice can serve as a lighthouse for others who want to realize their full potential, become more productive, and succeed spectacularly.

By honestly reviewing this book, you can serve as a source of inspiration for other people looking to develop self-control. Your words can inspire and motivate others, demonstrating that they possess the capacity to develop unbreakable habits, access the mental toughness of Navy SEALs, and adopt a monastic mindset for unrivaled productivity.

Consider how the lessons in "Self-Discipline" have changed you; share the most effective strategies you have used; consider the breakthroughs you have experienced; and consider the wonderful success you have attained. Others may be inspired by your review and be led down their path to self-discipline and a life of success.

Consider your review's effect on someone who has trouble focusing, being productive, or learning self-discipline. They can be motivated by your insight and genuineness to adopt the mentality and behaviors needed to excel in all facets of life.

Let's create a welcoming group committed to embracing self-discipline and realizing their greatest potential.

This is as easy as writing a review—a gesture that takes only a few seconds but has a big impact.

Your review can spark the pursuit of excellence and personal empowerment.

I appreciate you sharing your experience, wisdom, and suggestions. I wish you true self-discipline, unmatched focus, and extraordinary success on your journey to embracing self-discipline and achieving excellence in work, relationships, and life!

Thanks.

4
Cultivating A Monk Mindset

I am not and will never be a Zen monk. However, I am greatly inspired by how they try to live their lives: the simplicity of their existence, the focus and attention of each activity, and their peace and tranquility throughout the day.

You don't want to become a Zen monk, but you may follow simple guidelines to live a more Zen-like existence.

Why should you lead a more Zen-like life? Because who among us couldn't benefit from a bit more awareness, peace, and attention in their lives? Because Zen monks have spent their lives for hundreds of years serving others, being present in whatever they do, and being dedicated. Because it serves as a model for how we should live, and it is not important if we achieve this ideal.

It doesn't get any easier than that, according to Thich Nhat Hanh, one of my favorite Zen monks: "Smile, breathe, and go slowly."

However, I thought I'd share some of the strategies I've found to be effective in my experiments with Zen-like living for anyone who might like a little more detail. I am neither even a Zen Buddhist nor am I a Zen master. Nevertheless, I've discovered that certain ideas may be applied to any life, regardless of your religious convictions or standard of living.

Understanding The Principles Of A Monk's Mindset

So many factors outside of ourselves influence our thoughts, for better or worse. Monks separate themselves from society to carry out their responsibilities under common law and obedience while dedicating their lives to spiritual pursuits.

Buddhist monks typically live in monasteries alongside other monks as a community. Buddhists claim their teachings lead to the community's protection and prosperity.

Monks are given free food and permitted to go about their city on trains and buses, making them quite unique.

What can these unique individuals offer us about leading better lives? Buddhist monks are completely self-supporting; as a result, all they do is gratuitous and for the benefit of society.

I'm not advocating that you be seen as a good person; you must spend your entire life volunteering and giving back to your community.

If you look at this closely, you'll see that everything you do in life should come from a place of goodness. You shouldn't do deeds solely to gain a benefit, such as money or status.

Do things because they make you feel good to do them and because you think they are right.

Live Your Life's Purpose

Find out why you were placed on this planet and live your life purposefully. This is the secret to happiness. What brings you joy? Money? Status? Serving people well?

When you know this, devote your time to activities enabling you to live intentionally and achieve your life's mission. Be in the company of like-minded individuals who will help you realize your full potential.

We can design the life we want. Nobody else will work for what we want. If we don't, thus we won't get it.

We will be more content with the results if we put more effort into reaching our goals.

Overcome Your Fears

Buddhism holds that our pain is a result of our fear. What is the traditional Buddhist method for getting over fear? While there are many ways to overcome our fears, mindfulness is the basic Buddhist precept.

Sitting down in full silence and giving yourself time to be present in the moment is one of the simplest ways to eliminate fear and stress.

Prepare to feel your body and mind relax in a few minutes by concentrating all your focus and energy on that instant. Because fear is such a taxing emotion, we can use that energy to experience something more uplifting instead.

Only in the here and now can life be found. If we do not return to ourselves in the present moment, we cannot be in touch with life because the past is gone, and the future is not yet here.

Be more in control of your breathing the next time you're stressed. Knowing this can give you more control over how you react to fear and other stressful situations.

When you confront your fear, it loses its influence over you. Although fear is often the cause of our avoidance of conflict, this is the key to permanently overcoming our fear in general.

Simple Living

Buddhism teaches monks that happiness can be attained with minimal necessities. The neighborhood residents provide the monks with food, medicine, and robes. We can try to be more minimalistic if monks can live such a basic lifestyle to this degree.

Aside from receiving all of their necessities from society, Buddhist monks lived a simple existence because they believed that nothing was permanent and that accumulating too many things would only cause them to suffer. This is accurate.

Friendships, love affairs, and things bought from Amazon never last a lifetime. When we come to this realization too late, life becomes challenging, and it is challenging to let go.

When you own less stuff, you usually find that the world and your environments excite you more than material possessions. One thing that has enabled me to trade material possessions for experiences and helped me become a minimalist is traveling.

According to research, having a cluttered life reduces productivity and increases the likelihood that you'll think your life is a disaster.

An untidy room can impact our stress levels and decision-making processes. I can recall when my room was a complete disaster, and I was experiencing daily bouts of extreme depression and hopelessness.

After cleaning my room the following day, I felt better, more inspired, and more determined to finish things.

Practice Being Detached

What does it mean to be emotionally detached? Simply put, detachment is a technique for separating your emotions from a problem. While this doesn't require you to give up what you adore, it supports the adage, "Don't put all your eggs in one basket."

For Buddhist monks, detachment is not merely a way of coping with unpleasant emotions but a way of life.

Because nothing lasts forever, try not to focus all your time and effort on one subject. Even if you leave your middle school teaching position, you are still a teacher even though you are no longer employed there.

Don't let difficult circumstances cause you to lose who you are. Because they wish to spare themselves misery, monks avoid giving anything too many emotions and sensations.

Don't let a person or a job possess you. This is the appeal of detachment training. Take pleasure in the here and now and the good things that happen to you, but let the bad things go and let the bad feelings go.

Practices To Achieve Mental Clarity And Reduce Stress

Your mind is completely engaged and active while you are in a condition of mental clarity. We require mental clarity to solve issues and be productive throughout the day.

Despite all the difficulties posed by poor mental clarity, there are numerous strategies for encouraging attentive engagement. It can be made better for you.

All eight simple strategies for increasing mental clarity can be easily added to your daily routine. They can help you lay the groundwork for a clear, active, and bright mind. Additionally, if you are working with someone who appears to be losing mental clarity, encourage them to take care of themselves and direct them to resources that can help them.

1. Obtain Plenty Of Quality Sleep

Your energy level during the day strongly relates to how much sleep you obtain. Both mental and physical energy are affected by this.

You can prevent fatigue from building up and ensure that your mental performance is at its peak throughout the day if you adopt a regular and healthy sleeping regimen. A sleep tracker is one approach to monitoring your sleep routine and ensuring you receive enough good sleep.

2. Inhibit Your Stress

Your ability to think clearly will improve if you successfully minimize stress.

Finding individualized techniques for stress relief and relaxation is part of stress management. Additionally, you can monitor your daily stress levels with stress tracker gadgets.

You can maintain mental acuity and realize your best potential by being conscious of your stress levels.

3. Practice Being Mindful

Living in the moment is the beautiful art of mindfulness. You can better control your energy by slowing down and being aware of your surroundings, body, and activities.

4. Strive For Work-Life Harmony

Time for both work and leisure is necessary for a healthy work-life balance. Spending too much time at the office may cause you to lose energy and feel burned out.

Similarly, very few activities would get completed if all your attention was on unwinding and enjoying yourself. Understanding how to increase mental clarity and strike a healthy balance between work and life.

5. Exercise Self-Care

Self-care routines are a crucial component of existence. You'll be able to manage your stress levels and continue working if you can identify the resources, pursuits, environments, and people that give you a sense of security and support.

It's beneficial to your mental health to set aside time each week to do something you enjoy. Additionally, it will maintain your thinking resilient and adaptive.

6. Become Active

A fundamentally crucial component of good health — emotionally and physically — is moving your body regularly.

Sweating off impurities and energizing the circulatory system can keep the mind sharp. You can help yourself achieve mental clarity by engaging in simple physical activities like walking, swimming, or virtual yoga.

7. Keep A Balanced Diet

That's right; you can eat your way to a sharper mind. A good diet is essential for general health because of the intimate connection between nutrition and mental health.

There are many foods for mental clarity available that can provide you with all the nutrients required to build mental toughness.

The healthiest nutrients for the brain include berries, dark leafy greens, fatty salmon, and pumpkin seeds. Your brain will work at its best if you drink lots of water.

8. Seek Assistance

Many people find it difficult to reach out when they're struggling. However, one of the most empowering things a person can do is ask for assistance.

It's common to feel stressed and experience mental fogginess. Never be embarrassed to seek assistance from friends, relatives, or a medical expert. They will make you feel understood and recognized.

Balancing Productivity With Mindfulness And Presence

Mindfulness can greatly enhance our routines and thinking, whether at work or playing. People who practice mindfulness and are fully present have better relationships and are more likely to think creatively. Therefore, practicing mindfulness can also enhance your social life, interests, and job.

The benefits of mindfulness for productivity are plain to see. Just like plants need water, nutrition, and sunlight to grow, our thoughts require specific conditions too. Mindfulness cultivates these circumstances by eliminating stress-inducing emotions and distractions to sharpen focus, which is advantageous for any task requiring concentration.

By putting the mindfulness tips listed below into action, you'll find that you can accomplish more each day without working longer hours.

Get Into Your Meditation Mindset

Since mindfulness is typically a new way of thinking, it requires practice before it can be used. Building mindfulness muscle through meditation in all its forms is highly recommended. There is no right or wrong method to meditate; focusing on the here and now and your thoughts as they pass through your mind is necessary.

Try focusing on your breathing if you're new to meditation and need a place to begin. Simple and effective, the 4-7-8 breathing technique involves inhaling for four seconds, holding for seven, and then exhaling for eight. All the while, keep your attention on your breathing.

As an alternative, think about easing into meditation by installing an app like Headspace or Calm. Once you've identified your approach, incorporate it into your daily routine by pausing occasionally to refocus.

Do One Thing At A Time

In a society that values efficiency, we often choose multitasking as a short-term solution when we have much to do. However, juggling multiple things in practice causes unneeded tension as we battle to focus, which undoubtedly doesn't lighten your workload.

The most productive approach to work is to commit to one thing at a time during busy times. With a more attentive attitude, you can avoid stress and distractions by being fully present in what you're doing. You'll finish it more quickly, and the final product will be of greater quality.

Disconnect Every Day

We are continuously connected to social media and news websites. It might be difficult to unclutter one's mind when there is a constant barrage of media and information, which can be overpowering.

In the highly connected digital age, practicing mindfulness is often as easy as setting aside time without your phone or other electronic gadget. You should try to do something every day that doesn't include using an electronic gadget, whether inside or outside. Make dinner for some friends or go for a walk, but make sure everyone leaves their phones at the entrance!

Make A Distraction-Free Work Environment

Today's world is full of distractions, but you can manage them by creating the optimal working environment. Turn off all your devices' notifications when working or studying, and set up specific times to respond to emails and other work-related messages. Even a brief message can abruptly stop someone from paying attention.

Listening to music while working is advised as long as it's proper. According to Cambridge Sound Management research, 48% of office workers are easily distracted by speech; hence lyricless music is the best choice to maintain concentration. Make a playlist of music that helps you concentrate, or listen to one of the many collections available on Spotify or SoundCloud.

Order Up, Work Down

A key component of effective and mindful working is maximizing your attention span. You can accomplish this by prioritizing, categorizing, and scheduling your daily tasks according to priority, amount of focus required, and projected time. Since most people are alert and focused in the morning, starting with tasks requiring more mental energy is a smart choice.

Work your way down the list to end the day with the easiest jobs. This way, your day will naturally come to a close, and you'll feel at ease as your mental activity wanes.

Keep In Mind Why You Started

If you ever find yourself stuck on a task at work or in your studies, take a step back and remind yourself of why you are doing it. You'll be reminded of a broader purpose that can be overlooked among the difficult but necessary procedures required to complete a task by looking at the bigger picture.

Take some time to consider the moments during the day's work when you were challenged, informed, or inspired. When you need inspiration, write them down and refer to them later.

Move Forward!

It takes the cooperation of the body and mind to create mental clarity. Because of this, developing holistic mindfulness necessitates paying attention to the entire body.

If you can, use your work breaks to move your body physically. For example, you can juggle, go for a brisk walk, or throw a ball with a friend for 10 minutes. These activities will temporarily break up your strong concentration and clear some mental space, which will help you regain your focus when you return to the subject at hand.

Establishing mindful working habits will increase your productivity and reveal your greatest skills, whether you have examinations or a project deadline coming up. Become more focused and start working more efficiently!

5
Strengthening Self-Discipline In Business

Do you wish to launch a successful small business of your own? Or expand your current business? Perhaps you want to increase your productivity at work but don't want to own and operate a business.

"I could do that," you tell yourself. Why haven't you, then?

Any of these tasks will require self-discipline for you to complete. It seems so easy. But before you stop reading and assume you already know what you need to do, we bet there are a few self-discipline techniques and tricks you've probably never seen. Worth spending a few more minutes on?

Ironically, maintaining self-discipline is harder than it seems. Nevertheless, it's crucial to your success.

There is much to be said in the entrepreneurial setting simply by arriving on time and prepared to work. One stands out from the crowd like an alien spaceship parked in an Iowa cornfield simply by keeping deadlines and promises. Your ability to complete tasks appropriately the first time will draw great contacts, opportunities, and resources. Self-discipline is the key to everything here.

Your life can change for the better if you have self- discipline. Imagine how much you could do if you genuinely followed through on your goals and accomplished every task you set out to undertake. Your unrealized potential very well may be unlocked through self-discipline.

Building The Necessary Discipline To Become An Entrepreneur

Being an entrepreneur has many positive side effects, including becoming your boss, setting your hours, and finally operating the business of your dreams. However, becoming an entrepreneur is a goal that requires a lot of tenacity and self-discipline to accomplish, and not everyone is cut out to run a firm.

There are actions you can do to develop your self-discipline and get ready for the arduous journey ahead if you believe that entrepreneurship is the appropriate career route for you. Find out how to develop self-discipline and why it is important for success as a future business leader in the following nine tips.

1. Be Persistent And Patient

Numerous failures and setbacks in life will put you to the test, but you must keep moving forward regardless of your past performance. You'll eventually create a routine and a strategy to keep you motivated if you keep your eye on your ultimate goal. I start each morning with a routine and include timeboxing in my project management system to stay focused and maximize my time.

2. Identify Your Distractions

I define discipline as the ability to focus despite external distractions. You must recognize the obstacles that prevent you from developing self-discipline and take steps to change them so they do not recur. For instance, turning off my phone is crucial when I need to focus and be as productive as possible.

3. Prioritize What's Important Over What's Urgent

To me, self-discipline entails setting aside time daily to prioritize the important over the urgent. Every day, urgent issues arise in both our professional and personal life. But if I have set aside time in my calendar to concentrate on what matters to me and my business, I can go forward much more quickly.

4. Respond To Any Procrastination

Consider the causes of your procrastination if you lack discipline. Procrastination is an emotion regulation issue rather than a problem with time management or self-discipline. Find a trend; you are probably continually putting off certain things. Are you scared of failing, or are you just plain bored? Once you identify the problem, you can take immediate action.

5. Take Baby Steps At First

Successful entrepreneurs tend to be harsh on themselves. They must possess the capacity for extended hours of effort, resilience, and long-term thinking. It's crucial, to begin with baby steps while trying to develop self-discipline. If you want to work continuously for longer than an hour without taking a break, try setting a timer. Build up your self-discipline gradually by starting small.

6. Postpone Gratification

Be responsible and content without needing immediate gratification. Sometimes we discipline ourselves into believing we are ready for another reward. With the understanding that there is still work to be done and the reward will take time, try to put off everything—especially your "wants"—and see how long you can endure. As a bonus, you'll gain perseverance and patience.

7. Establish And Adhere To A Schedule

Making and adhering to your timetable is one method for developing self-discipline. New business owners don't bother creating a defined schedule because they think they must work at least 50 hours each week to be successful. You can complete the same work in 30 to 40 hours if disciplined. I advise picking a six- to eight-hour work block corresponding to your highest production levels.

8. Maintain A Daily To-Do List

Keep an organized list of your daily tasks. This will help you track what needs to be done, create a schedule, and prioritize tasks. I record my tasks separately by date in my calendar app to ensure I don't forget anything. This will help you stay organized and responsible.

9. Change Your Mindset

It takes self-discipline to honor commitments to oneself. Only after failing at self-discipline hundreds of thousands of times can one become an expert. Be kind to yourself, and remember you are only responsible for helping yourself. This paradigm change significantly lessens the bad feelings and thoughts that come with failure and gives you the confidence to keep trying despite failure.

Strategies For Effective Time Management And Goal Setting

You can create and achieve SMART goals to enhance your overall time management by following these seven steps:

1. Create A SMART Goal

You can add structure to your day by using SMART goals to help you with time management since you can clearly outline your goals and follow the format to finish them on time. When creating a SMART goal for time management, try outlining the goal by responding to the following questions:

Specific: What am I trying to achieve?

Measurable: How will I be able to tell when I've succeeded? What elements can be measured?

Attainable: Is this goal reachable given my abilities, finances, and the amount of work I still have to do?

Relevance: How does this goal fit into the general priorities I have?

Time: When do I hope to achieve this goal?

2. Establish A List

After establishing your SMART goal, think about making a list to help you concentrate on what you must perform to meet your deadline. For instance, if the deadline for your goal is in a month, create a step-by-step list with bigger weekly targets. This will provide a framework to help you manage each process phase.

From there, you can list more manageable weekly goals to help you reach the larger one. Try making a list of daily tasks that need to be accomplished the following day after each day to aid in time management. Since you've previously planned your day's tasks, the list could help you stay focused when you start your day.

3. Set Aside Time On Your Calendar

You can utilize a tool to block time on your daily calendar once you've made your lists. Setting aside specific blocks of time will let you stay on task throughout the day and prevent interruptions from other work. It's a useful tool because you can schedule things according to particular times using the list you made. You can prioritize the more difficult tasks at the start of your day and save the easier tasks for the finish.

4. Delegate Tasks

At work, assign responsibilities to others whenever you can. Doing this lets you convey to your coworkers that you value and trust them. Additionally, it enables you to take advantage of other people's talents and skills to do the necessary tasks. By delegating tasks to others, you can lower your stress level and increase productivity in other activities, like handling customer complaints or filing performance reports.

5. Get Rests

Setting aside time for breaks during the day is crucial to time management. Setting aside time for non-work-related activities is crucial to prevent being tired from working too much. Outside of lunch, you might want to plan time-specific breaks that allow you to concentrate on things other than work. Snack, take a brief stroll, or use your phone. Whatever you decide, taking a break from tasks that are just relevant to your job can improve the quality of your work.

6. Do Not Be Distracted

Since it's easy to become sidetracked when working, strive to eliminate any distractions preventing you from finishing a project on time. Common distractions include using cell phones, checking irrelevant emails, engaging in pointless chats with coworkers, or streaming music or films in the background. Concentrating on each task is usually much easier once you remove these distractions. You can improve your productivity and effectiveness at work by establishing limits and eliminating these distractions.

7. Concentrate On One Task At Once

Many people try to multitask during the workday to finish things, but concentrating on one thing at a time allows you to give that task all of your attention. Concentrating on one activity at a time instead of several at once usually enhances the overall pace at which you do the task and yields higher-quality outcomes.

6
Mastering Self-Discipline In Relationships

Men and women are meant to be two halves combined to become one whole. They each possess unique traits and features that, when correctly combined, produce the completion, equilibrium, and harmony that nature needs. Respect and trust are the pillars of a successful marriage and meaningful relationships.

A successful marriage necessitates a great deal of self-control and discipline. Love necessitates selflessness and giving. The pleasure and wellbeing of the other person take precedence over your own when you are truly in love with them. When someone is loved, one is prepared to make sacrifices for their welfare.

No matter how close you feel to one other and how compatible you may be in many aspects, there will always be areas of discord, unhappiness, and discontent when two people get into a romantic relationship. Being transparent and honest is a must for self-discipline in a relationship. Honesty necessitates the ability to express one's thoughts and feelings without becoming agitated or angry, as well as the ability to listen patiently and calmly to the thoughts, feelings, and opinions of others.

The Importance Of Self-Discipline In Relationships

Every relationship must be able to handle certain situations, whether they are positive or negative. A couple's ability to handle the dynamics of certain situations can make or break their relationship. Many relationships break down today because of unmet emotional demands that a spouse may have been carrying from adolescence into adulthood, finally finding the ideal place to be unloaded and someone to blame.

Have you ever questioned why certain couples can maintain a happy and long-lasting marriage even after spending decades together? It is feasible to complete and is not particularly difficult. Simple self-discipline and prioritizing one another's happiness over other considerations are all required. Self-discipline is characterized as regulating your thoughts, feelings, and behaviors; it is crucial for maintaining any positive and tranquil relationship.

Self-Discipline Encourages Compassion

Relationships, especially marriages, will inevitably have conflicts. The marriage may be strained when this happens, and the couple's children and young adults may experience emotional stress. This may result from a lack of self-discipline and an inability to identify each other's strengths and shortcomings before your marriage is in danger of disintegrating.

Understanding your wants and the opportunities available to you allows you to address those needs without venting your conflicts or problems to other people.

Couples can only have a successful marriage if they know their identities, primary life goals, and marriage aspirations. Most marital disagreements grow because one or both partners cannot regulate their emotions appropriately and often overreact even to the smallest events. Impulsive verbal exchanges might spark an emotional storm and result in irrational behavior.

Self-Discipline Defines Reactions

Your mental and exterior behavior can greatly impact the lives of those around you; thus, self-discipline is very important. Women have a reputation for exercising self-discipline; logically, their brains are more suited to controlling their emotions than men. But in today's world, where feminism has found a place, more women are becoming more receptive to circumstances. In the presence of injustice and inequality, certain women can experience triggers. Exercising self-control is also essential. Be mindful of your behavior, how it may affect others, and your goal.

Self-Discipline Promotes Mindfulness

Some couples split up because they cannot envision their future as a couple, especially when the present appears overwhelming and unfathomable. Others dream of a stress-free marriage but are ill-equipped to make the sacrifices necessary to make things work when things go wrong. Any successful marriage depends on the ability of the partners to look ahead to the future together, even when the present appears unclear. The likelihood of an unhappy marriage increases when one partner struggles to remain optimistic in the heat of the moment. Self-restrained partners are more likely to practice patience, become sensitive to one another's sentiments, and be able to strike a balance between their aspirations and the long-term advantages of preserving the marriage.

Communication Skills To Build Strong Connections

You must let down your guard and regularly work to convey your feelings to learn how to have a healthy and honest relationship.

Healthy communication skills are incomplete without paying close attention to what your spouse is saying. This will make it easier for you to comprehend their needs and feelings.

The next stage is to take actions that encourage communication between you and your spouse after you have taken the time to understand why communication is crucial in relationships.

The following relationship communication techniques will help you save your marriage:

Focus On Your Partner

Never chat while texting. Give your spouse your full attention, whether they are cracking a joke or sharing a sensitive family matter.

Put aside any devices that might be distracting, mute or turn off the TV, and lean closer to your companion. This will demonstrate your concern for their privacy to them. Excellent techniques to demonstrate that you are paying attention to your spouse include nodding and keeping eye contact.

Designate a space in your home where the electronics can be kept to reduce technology distractions.

Don't Interrupt Your Partner

The quickest way to start a fight is to be interrupted. It's critical that both you and your spouse feel heard and allowed to speak when talking.

Even if you think your partner is mistaken about a fact, jumping in with your opinion may be alluring while they are still speaking. However, it is crucial to wait.

Your lover will respect you more if you pay them full attention while focusing and connecting. Maintaining communication skills in interpersonal relationships requires doing this.

Build A Neutral Space

Relationship communication skills development might be difficult. Many couples find it helpful to discuss "tough" marital issues in a neutral space, like the kitchen table.

Assaulting your spouse by bringing up their lack of sexual prowess while already feeling vulnerable can make them see the bedroom poorly in the future.

Another instance of one party believing they had the proverbial "high ground" in the disagreement is arguing in a relative's home.

Talk To Them Directly

Consistently having face-to-face conversations about significant issues is one of the best communication techniques you can do in relationships. Since the tone of voice cannot be discerned through text messages, texting is undoubtedly not the place to have meaningful conversations about romantic relationships or to make important decisions.

Instead, pick a moment to speak to your partner face to face. This will enable you to focus on and understand one another's nonverbal signs fully. There is little chance of something becoming "lost in translation" through technology when something is communicated in person.

When Issues Occur, Use "I" Statements

When couples argue, one issue they encounter is attacking one another. You relieve your partner of some responsibility by employing "I" phrases.

Instead of saying, "You did this, and it made me angry," try expressing, "I feel that when this happened, my feelings were hurt."

See the difference? Instead of criticizing your partner for the issue, you took it upon yourself.

This easy-to-use but powerful tactic stops either of you from launching an attack or raising your defenses unnecessarily.

Be Sincere With Your Partner

Being truthful is not always easy, but essential to a successful relationship. Telling your partner when you believe an issue requires discussion is one example of being honest. It also entails owning up to your mistakes and expressing regret rather than creating excuses.

Being honest with your partner not only promotes open and sincere conversation but it also helps establish trust. This is one of the most crucial methods of communicating in relationships.

Discuss The Little Things

One of the best communication skills is discussing small and significant issues with your partner. You might improve your marriage by sharing humorous stories from your week or talking about your day and feelings.

Every topic should be up for conversation once you get married. Nothing should be too uncomfortable or awkward to communicate. Talking about the small problems now will make it easier to discuss bigger issues later.

Apply The 24-Hour Rule

There will inevitably be difficulties when two people live together and are married.

When your lover is nearby, you could experience some days when rainbows and butterflies glide through your house. Sometimes when your spouse is nearby, you'll start to experience headaches.

If you are ready to complain to your partner because you are angry with them, hold off. Use the 24-hour rule as a guide.

So, he didn't pick up his socks, or she didn't empty the dishwasher. Is the world coming to an end? In a day, will it still matter to you? If not, you might want to let it go.

Make Physical Contact

Maintaining physical contact is crucial regardless of how you conduct your conversation. Oxytocin is released more readily in response to low-intensity skin stimulation, such as touching or stroking a partner's arm.

In addition to fostering empathy and bonding between romantic partners, the love hormone can reduce stress and foster cooperative behavior.

Funnel Out Communication

Discussing problems and their solutions, family and financial issues, and how you and your spouse conclude are all examples of communication. But keep in mind that talking should be enjoyable as well.

Talking with your partner entails sharing humorous stories and future aspirations and engaging in thoughtful discussion. Oxytocin and dopamine increase, and a deeper emotional connection is made during these times.

Whether the talk that follows is serious or lighthearted, always take the time to check in with your partner vocally.

7
Sustaining Self-Discipline For Life - Embracing The Journey

Numerous significant traits might boost someone's success and happiness, but only one produces long-lasting, sustained success in all facets of life: self-discipline. Self-discipline is the most important quality needed to achieve goals, maintain a healthy lifestyle, and ultimately be happy. This is true regardless of how you feel about your nutrition, fitness, work ethic, or relationships.

A study found that people with strong self-discipline are happier than those without it. The study confirmed this since the disciplined participants were better able to manage goal conflicts. These individuals could make wise selections more quickly and spend less time contemplating whether to engage in unhealthy habits. The disciplined did not allow feelings or impulses to control their decisions. Instead, they avoided feeling anxious or agitated and made informed, logical judgments daily.

Contrary to popular belief, developing self-discipline is a learned behavior. It demands regular repetition and practices in your daily life. Try the tried-and-true techniques in this chapter for improved control to strengthen your self-discipline. This program will help you create positive habits, destroy negative ones, and improve your ability to manage by making little adjustments to your daily routine. Your life will be more liberated if you have more self-discipline since it will enable you to make rational choices rather than emotional ones. Have a go at it. You'll be grateful for it when you're happy.

Maintaining Discipline In The Face Of Distractions

Maintaining discipline during the workday more difficult than ever? It's not just you. Distractions come in all forms, from pings, notifications, and emails to coworkers who share your anxiety about the outside world and pinging, notifications, and emails. The situation has gotten worse as more businesses transition to remote workforces. Since there are more distractions than ever, how do you maintain discipline?

Your organization's productivity efforts pay off in employee satisfaction beyond the financial benefits: studies show that people with self-discipline are happier than those easily lost amid distractions. If you're chasing ROI, it's worth investing your time and attention toward discipline amid distraction (both for yourself and your team!). You'll become happier if you practice discipline at work and save time and energy.

It requires a lot of skill to propel your organization through transformation. No matter the workplace setting, using these self-discipline techniques can help you stay on track. You'll be prepared to share with your team as you incorporate these into your workflow.

<u>Create Job Cues</u>

Let's be honest. We are accustomed beings. Our brains require a small cue that it is time to start working. You'll focus better and take more action if you establish signs that indicate it's time to concentrate. Examine your average day and determine what helps you stay focused and what doesn't. There's a chance that subconscious thoughts are diverting your mind.

Even if you don't have any video calls scheduled for the day, getting "dressed" and prepared for the camera is a good idea. This habitual action serves as a quick reminder to get to work.

Closing the office door, putting on headphones, or playing a playlist of job-related music are further cues to get you in the work mood. Make it a routine to think about what gets your brain working. Share the advantages with your team when you use these in your workflow so they can do the same.

<u>Establish Priorities</u>

An employee is interrupted 50 to 60 times on average per day. Priorities are crucial because there is still work to be done. Setting specific goals can increase achievement, lessen stress, organize the day, and help you respond sensibly to requests. You might be amazed by how much better your day will be once you set priorities and organize your work and how much better your colleagues' days will be once they have the tools necessary to do the same.

Once you've written or typed out your tasks, rank them. What needs to be done right away? What will still matter even when it's not as urgent? You have a defined workflow so you can avoid distractions. You might review your priorities again to decide what must be done immediately and what can wait.

Take Planned But Flexible Breaks

You are probably familiar with the Pomodoro Technique, which calls for a five-minute break after every 25 minutes of work. Your workflow can require a different strategy when you're in a leadership position and need to be reachable. Everybody approaches discipline and diversion differently. The secret is to plan your breaks carefully while remaining adaptable to what the day brings.

Last-minute meetings or pressing activities could disrupt scheduled breaks, but pausing is still crucial. You'll be less productive if you never "off" your work mode. The ability to concentrate on shorter, higher-quality work sessions (instead of nonstop, subpar labor) demonstrates to your staff what long-term success looks like.

Give yourself a break from the internal judgment when life interferes, and take a big breath. Think of your deliberate breaks as an example for your team. If you take a brief mental break, your staff will observe that they can do the same.

Set Yourself Up For Success

Your day's conclusion sets the tone for your morning routine. It could be tempting to change course and stop doing everything. When you start your day, intentionally preparing for the following day's job can make all the difference. Before leaving the office, establish your priorities for the next day.

You can successfully go to work the following morning with just a few minutes of preparation the previous evening. With this planning, you'll know exactly what's most crucial and be ready to get started immediately rather than getting lost in a disorganized inbox.

Whether a crisis is present or not, your team will benefit from your leadership skills. Optimal leadership techniques could increase productivity in the average organization by 50%. Imagine how much of a difference it could make in difficult circumstances if your leadership is more effective in good times.

You can develop self-discipline by using new methods to stay focused amid distractions. Your effect will change as you do, and your staff will have the tools they need to be successful.

Strategies For Self-Reflection And Continuous Improvement

Self-reflection entails taking the time to consider and assess your behavior and personality. This entails taking stock of your ideas, actions, values, prejudices, reasons for acting the way you do, and goals. Finding the "why" behind your ideas, feelings, and actions is what this process entails.

Now that you understand what it entails let's get started with some practical advice for incorporating self-reflection into your life.

Ask Questions To Encourage Reflection

Try to come up with some questions you can ask yourself to encourage self-reflection. You can establish a habit of self-reflection by having prepared questions. Try using this daily, weekly, or monthly routine—whatever works for you!

To encourage self-reflection, this is a fantastic place to start. You can learn a lot about yourself by thoughtfully responding to some of these questions.

Journal

Writing in a journal is a great way to express your feelings. You can use it to reflect and identify trends and changes in your reflections.

Many excellent tools are available to help you if you need assistance getting started or are unsure what to write about. Try a paper journal or an online diary app for self-reflection and self-discovery.

The Ability To Discern Self-Reflection From Rumination

Although self-reflection is meant to be a positive and helpful process, there are instances when it deviates into worry, negativity, and rumination.

To make sure you are getting the most out of your thoughts, it is crucial to distinguish between helpful self-reflection and ruminating.

Reflective thoughts are intriguing but objective or factual.

For instance, ask yourself, "What drove me to do that? Why did I act in that manner? In contrast, ruminating thoughts typically tend to be more unfavorable, critical, and emotional. For example, 'I can't believe I did such a stupid thing; what is wrong with me?'

Pause and try again later if you start contemplating rather than reflecting. To stop ruminating, you can also try some of these suggestions.

Get Help

Self-reflection can occasionally be challenging to accomplish on your own. There is no shame in asking a loved one or a qualified professional for support if you need assistance processing challenging feelings or circumstances.

You can improve your capacity for self-reflection with the help of therapists in a secure setting. If you discover that ruminating is a problem, they can also help explore any underlying problems that might be a contributing cause.

Set Aside Time For Self-Reflection

Schedule time specifically for self-reflection to make it a priority! Life can get stressful with our phones buzzing continuously, new shows to binge-watch, social obligations, work, etc.

If you don't consciously set aside time for self-reflection, chances are you won't do it often enough to reap the rewards. Start with weekly or bimonthly intervals and work your way up to daily.

We miss the chance to develop and gain knowledge from our experiences when we don't self-reflect on our life. Self-reflection is an ability that needs to be nurtured and developed. You can incorporate self-reflective activities into your daily life and reap its numerous advantages with a little time and perseverance. Try one of the suggestions above as a small step, then build on that!

Career Milestones To Celebrate

It can be very thrilling and fulfilling to think of your professional life in terms of career milestones. By celebrating your achievements in your career, you increase your self-confidence, pride, and bravery and widen your horizons to new possibilities.

Career-defining moments occur every day. They can include finishing a project, landing the job, or receiving praise from the supervisor. Professionals often overlook smaller career milestones instead of concentrating primarily on the major ones, such as a new position or retirement.

But when you downplay less obvious or modest job achievements, you're robbing yourself of a tiny bit of your professional soul. Instead, appreciating each one gives you the internal drive you need to pursue and accomplish the next.

Set Achievement Goals To Reach Career Milestones

Setting goals for success is crucial. These goals can be major, like getting a promotion, or minor, like thirty uninterrupted minutes of focus time.

It is more important that you set achievement goals and pursue them than the size of your goals.

Even if you haven't achieved them all yet, taking steps toward them is important. It helps you in making progress toward both your career and personal success.

Having a clear career path makes success even easier to achieve. Only after you know your options can you pursue this career route.

So, enter the career progression map.

Map Your Career Development

A career growth map resembles a treasure map exactly as you can think. It is ultimately what you want to achieve this year, in five years, or at whatever time frame you have in mind.

Your ultimate goal may not be quite evident now, but it will become clearer as you progress. The key is to avoid becoming impatiently fixed while waiting for the result to be flawless. You must get moving!

A professional development map's goal is to help you identify your direction. This life path map, which includes career milestones from graduation to retirement, may serve as your guide.

This professional progression map's dynamic nature makes it intriguing. This map will include new and unexpected turns that appear along the journey. Additionally, keep in mind that your goals may change as you do.

Life also happens in parallel with your work advancement. In twenty years, what you want now can look completely different. That's alright.

If you're prepared to work hard and be adaptable, this job path will truly take you on a lifelong journey.

15 Professional Milestones To Celebrate

Are you prepared to begin? The following list of fifteen career milestones, both significant and minor, should serve as motivation:

Graduation, First Interview, Important Move, Inaugural Job, Next Job, Big Promotion, Noteworthy Projects, Day-to-Day Accomplishments, First Speech, Critical Conversations, Great Evaluation, Leadership Role, Boardroom Seat, Career Retirement, Encore Career.

When you reflect on your professional achievements, be proud of everything you've accomplished and remember the road fondly. There is still a long way to go, and certain milestones must be reviewed repeatedly. However, that is what adds interest and insight to the career experience.

Start recognizing your accomplishments and making plans for the important career milestones that lie ahead.

Conclusion

You have the right to be and lead the best life possible. Whether your goal is to heal your relationships, get promoted, lose weight, or achieve your goals, self-discipline is one of the most important components. Setting up good habits will benefit you both now and in the future.

Extending your comfort zone is the key to developing discipline. It needs constant dedication to focus.

It's challenging for everyone. Start small: work for 30 minutes, then take a five-minute break. As your body and mind acclimate, gradually extend your workday.

It makes no difference how you develop self-discipline, whether it involves reading books, listening to podcasts, consulting a mentor, or exercising personal diligence. You must be making efforts to develop positive behaviors.

We won't sugarcoat it; it's difficult to develop discipline. But if you're prepared to work hard, we'll be here for you every step of the way.

Start your journey to self-improvement now by developing better self-discipline. Your ability to exercise self-control will help you live a better life.

www.ingramcontent.com/pod-product-compliance
Lightning Source LLC
Chambersburg PA
CBHW022120090426
42743CB00008B/936